Happy special birthday
to my best friend
Wendy. I feel very
blessed to have a
friend like you. Love batty
xox

Published by Ronnie Sellers Productions, Inc.
Copyright © 2005 Ronnie Sellers Productions, Inc.
Artwork © Westland Giftware, Inc.
All rights reserved.
Illustrations by Mike Dowdall, Text by Pat Welch

Project Editor: Robin Haywood
Production Editor: Mary Baldwin
Design: Pat Welch

P.O. Box 818, Portland, Maine 04104
For ordering information:
Phone: (800) MAKE-FUN (625-3386) • Fax: (207) 772-6814
Visit our Web site: www.makefun.com • E-mail: rsp@rsvp.com

ISBN: 1-56906-586-1
Library of Congress Control Number: 2004195749

10 9 8 7 6 5 4 3 2 1

Printed and bound in the United States of America

Biddys™

illustrations by Mike Dowdall
text by Pat Welch

RONNIE SELLERS PRODUCTIONS, INC.

PORTLAND, MAINE

CONTENTS

The Biddy: An Introduction

She can be found in every part of the country – but her preferred habitats include Solvang, California, Saks Fifth Avenue, and Branson, Missouri. She is highly mobile, and may at any time be seen cruising along the nation's highways – at 45 mph in the fast lane. She knows the right fork to use, the correct composition of a thank-you note, and the difference between a doily and an antimacassar. She will gladly share this information with you. She is on a constant quest to improve her mind, and eagerly seeks the counsel of recognized experts – her astrologer, her psychic, her hairdresser. She is a world traveler, and is familiar with the languages and customs of many cruise ship lines. Her children are grown and gone from the nest; her husband has either retired to the golf course or gone to his spiritual reward – either is acceptable to her (and, for that matter, to him). She has reached the stage in life where her principal concern when selecting shoes is comfort, not style. A lifetime of reflection and observation, of filling the duties of wife, mother, counselor, helpmate, hostess, and maid, have culminated in the point of view with which she now approaches the world, which can be summed up in one phrase:

"It's my turn, honey."

The Biddy Primer

WHO THEY ARE, WHERE THEY
ARE, AND WHAT TO DO IF YOU SURPRISE ONE
IN HER NATURAL HABITAT

THE BIDDY TEST

It is commonly believed that one becomes a biddy by the ordinary circumstance of reaching a certain age. The truth, however, is that biddyhood is not merely reached. Rather, like other advanced states of mind, it is achieved.

But if age is not the sole determining factor, how is one to know when one is, in fact, in the presence of a biddy? For your convenience, we have provided the following simple test which you can administer to your subject. Instructions on interpreting the results are at the bottom of the facing page. It's true that they are printed upside down, but you should not take that to mean that you win anything for figuring that out.

The Biddy Test

1. The manners of today's children are not significantly inferior to those of a generation ago.

    ☐ True   ☐ False

2. The manners of today's adults are not significantly inferior to those of a generation ago.

    ☐ True   ☐ False

3. Most waiters do their best to provide prompt and courteous service.

    ☐ True   ☐ False

4. Somewhere in the world, there is a bathroom
which has been properly cleaned.

☐ True   ☐ False

5. It is more sensible to be comfortable than to wear
hose and gloves on a simple shopping trip.

☐ True   ☐ False

6. The concept of couples writing their own wedding
vows is a positive modern trend.

☐ True   ☐ False

7. The advance of useful technology did not end with
the invention of the telephone.

☐ True   ☐ False

8. Coasters, doilies, and antimacassars no longer serve
any important purpose.

☐ True   ☐ False

You have probably guessed that a real biddy will have answered "false" to all eight statements
(with the possible exception of number four, in which case she will mean her own) but this is not
the correct interpretation. Actually, it doesn't matter what answers your subject gave. If she allowed
you to accost her in public and push your papers at her without whacking you with her cane – or
at the very least telling you to tuck in your shirt and get a haircut – she is not what you are looking
for. The true biddy does not take "tests" from riffraff she encounters on the street.

RECOGNIZING THE BIDDY

Obviously, in any scientific study, it is important to be sure you are studying the right subject. There are, of course, many visual identifiers of the biddy, but not all of her defining characteristics are apparent on the outside. If some doubt remains even after visual examination, there is at least one other test which rarely fails: take the suspected biddy to lunch and use the wrong fork for your salad. If she does not mention your transgression, she is probably not a biddy.

Nothing says "Don't give a damn" like a really big hat.

Maximum size of dog is approximately the same as a commercial toaster. There is no minimum size.

Carries a cell phone in her purse, but never remembers to recharge it.

Jewelry she can't fit on herself usually goes here.

Once would endure anything to look good. Now buys shoes in her correct size.

Wears all her jewelry at all times because she knows some awful drug addict is breaking into her house this very minute.

Doesn't bother trying to fix whatever's chafing, because everything always feels like that anyway.

Decreased olfactory acuity means she wears enough perfume to stun small animals at twenty feet.

Biddys Across America

Haight-Ashbiddy

Biddy The Kid

Aloha Biddy

Palm Springs Biddy

GOP Biddy

Heartland Biddy

Beacon Hill Biddy

Bleecker St. Biddy

Antebellum Biddy

Beach Biddy

THE BIDDY COMMUNICATION NETWORK

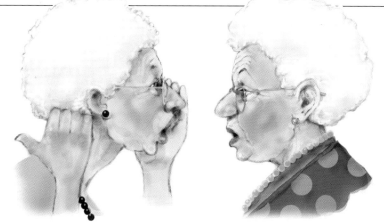

1 *"I just heard from Cynthia that her 19-year-old daughter is going to California to study the condor in its natural habitat to advance her bachelor's degree."*

2 *"Millie says Cynthia's daughter is going to California to study the habitats of 19 condors for some advanced bachelor."*

3 *"Daphne told me that Cynthia's daughter is moving to a condo in California to study the habits of 19 bachelors of advanced age."*

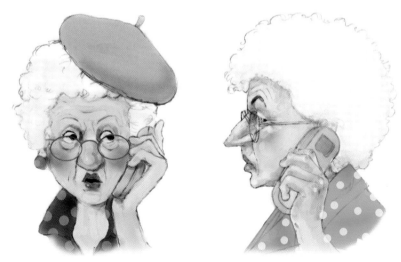

4 *"Alexis has heard for an absolute fact that Cynthia has run away to California and is living in a condo with a 19-year-old bachelor with bad habits who made advances. Can you imagine what her poor daughter must be going through?"*

Pookie and Snuffums

The special relationship which exists between the biddy and one variety or another of tiny, nervous dogs has been the subject of much discussion. Usually, it is attributed to "empty nest syndrome." The diminutive and helpless animals take the place of the children who once were totally dependent on the biddy but who have now grown up and left home.

But this theory loses credibility in light of the fact that the biddy, in her childrearing days, would have done anything to get a few hours away from the kids, while now she never goes anywhere without the dog. Only one conclusion fits the evidence:

This is not a dog, it's an accessory.

Mittens and Mr. Whiskers

Just as the tiny dogs typically associated with the biddy actually function more as fashion accessories than as dogs, the cats associated with a particular type of biddy serve a purpose other than simply being cats: they are collectibles. Like all collectibles, the apparent point is to amass a lot of them. And, like all collectibles, their principal value is as conversation pieces. Thus, the collector biddy may be easily identified by her conversation, which includes

such phrases as, "Fluffy sure lets me know if I forget to microwave her Tuna Bits," or "Snowball just thinks she's a person," or "You can't tell me Ming Toy doesn't understand every word I say."

Actually, her conversation doesn't just *include* such phrases. It consists of nothing but.

Biddy Finance 101

Dorothy had a chicken Caesar salad ($12.50), two glasses of Pinot Noir ($14.00), a slice of chocolate cheesecake ($8.25) and a half-caf low-foam soy latte ($4.75).

Esther had a Perrier with lemon ($4.00), chicken pot pie ($14.50), one glass of Sauvignon Blanc ($6.00), kiwi torte ($7.50) and coffee ($3.00).

Cynthia had plain water with lemon, an egg white and watercress omelette ($9.00), and decaf coffee with non-dairy creamer and sugar substitute ($3.00).

Amelia had two Bombay martinis ($13.00), a shrimp cocktail ($7.50), another Bombay martini ($6.50), sauteed sea scallops ($16.00), three glasses of Pinot Grigiot ($22.50), a bite of Dorothy's cheesecake and the remains of Esther's torte, coffee with a shot of dark rum ($8.00), and, what the hell, one more Bombay martini ($6.50).

As Cynthia studies the check, Amelia suggests, rather loudly, that they stop being such a bunch of little old ladies and just split it four ways. Since it is Cynthia's turn to organize the next lunch, she makes a mental note: reservations for three.

BIDDYSPEAK

The biddy's sense of propriety is not limited to table settings, grooming, or the discreet camouflage of such offensive objects as toasters and tissue boxes. She also strictly observes the rule, "If you can't say anything nice, then at least don't say everything you're *thinking*."

So this is your young man?
I thought you might at least do a little better than your mother did.

I'm sure Lenore's husband is enjoying his retirement.
Having a job must have occasionally cut into his drinking time.

It was so kind of you to come.
And to wear your second-best house dress.

I especially enjoyed your sermon on gluttony.
The gravy stain on your raiment hardly distracted at all.

It was lovely that they wrote their own vows.
It could only have been better if they had somehow mastered sixth-grade English.

I understand Sophia's taking a cruise this summer.
I suppose she finally went through all the men who actually live here.

I love what you've done with this room.
Edgar Alan Poe probably would have liked it too.

My dear, you must have gone down a full two sizes.
Amazing what you can do on a strict regimen of amphetamines and vodka.

BEAUTY AND THE BIDDY

DIET AND EXERCISE ARE ALL
WELL AND GOOD WHEN YOU'RE YOUNG,
BUT SURGERY IS FOREVER

The Bodacious Biddy

The biddy, who was inclined to flaunt it in her younger days, seems to be — if anything — even more so inclined after she has reached biddyhood. As the biddy herself is likely to express it, "I still got it, honey. It's all just a little lower than it used to be."

This exhibitionist tendency has often been the cause of great consternation among more traditional biddys, and has been the motivation for more than one daughter to take an extended post-graduate sabbatical in India. But when it comes to the husbands, even the most bodacious biddy's behavior seems to be not only tolerated, but actively encouraged.

THE BIDDY AND HER BODY

As we have seen, the biddy is no stranger to the concept of putting a positive spin on certain unpleasant realities. For this reason, she does not consider that her skin has lost elasticity, but rather that it has gained character; not that her flesh has sagged, but that it has settled in a pleasing manner. And if she has become somewhat wrinkled – and the tiniest bit spotted and blotched – these small inconveniences are more than compensated for by the wisdom and sophistication she has developed over the years.

Besides, while it may be true that the mirror doesn't lie, it is also true that one sees what one wants to see, and one always has the option of not looking.

MOTHER NATURE'S LITTLE HELPERS

The average biddy does not have a vain bone in her body. Still, she feels that it is incumbent upon one to look one's best on all occasions, and there are times when one could use a little help along those lines. Help, of course, is available in many forms and to many degrees. Some biddys use little more than an eyebrow pencil and a dab of blush, while others may take advantage of the less extreme cosmetic medical procedures, such as occasional injections of Botox or collagen. But, as in any group, there is a small minority who believes in going for broke, and it is in this group that you will find the biddy who has been rebuilt from scratch as often as the transmission of a '72 Volkswagen.

1. A little Botox to smooth out that frown line. As if she hadn't earned it, after forty years of marriage to that old fool.

2. A tiny tuck to perk up those droopy eyelids. Not that there's anything all that worth seeing nowadays.

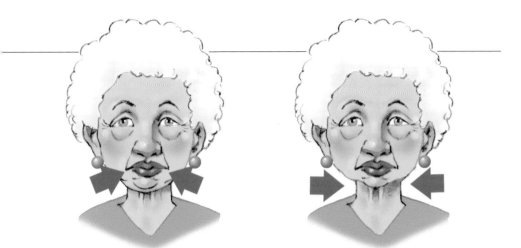

3. A smidge of collagen to plump up the lips. And if that old letch Horace Stymington makes another move, he's going to need a new pair of Depends.

4. Some minor work to firm up the chin and neck. When certain people need to be spoken to harshly, one doesn't like to wobble excessively.

5. While we're at it, might as well go after that jawline. Jowls are for bulldogs and prime ministers, and she doesn't have much use for either.

6. Occasionally she throws caution to the wind and does it all. The results, if we are to judge by appearances, are often quite surprising.

THE RIGHT HAIR

The biddy is extremely conscientious in all matters of dress and grooming, but she knows that it all means nothing if you don't have the Right Hair. The exact definition of the Right Hair has been established over many generations, but has only been truly perfected in the last fifty years or so – a period during which it is generally agreed that the greatest social advance was the availability of cheap and plentiful hair spray. Many nuances of color and style are acceptable (it is essential to the biddy to be able to express her individuality), but the principal criteria for the Right Hair are that it must smell like a five-gallon drum of shellac and have the surface density of a fiberglass boat hull.

Nothing promotes self-confidence like knowing you have the Right Hair.

Achieving the Right Hair takes time and magazines. The biddy has plenty of both.

THE BIDDY AND HER DOCTOR

The biddy understands that her relationship with her doctor — like her relationship with any number of other expert advisors, such as her attorney, her minister, her stockbroker, and her psychic — must be based on mutual trust and respect. But the biddy also understands (as many of her advisors do not) that "trust and respect" are euphemisms for power and intimidation. This is why the biddy prefers that her doctor be no more than a year or two out of medical school – not because he has the most up-to-date education, but because she knows, and he knows she knows, that psychologically speaking, she is going to turn him every way but loose.

THE MOBILE BIDDY

IF YOU DON'T THINK TRAVEL
IS BROADENING, SPEND A FEW DAYS AT AN
ALL-YOU-CAN-EAT BUFFET ON A CRUISE SHIP

BIDDYS ON WHEELS

For most of her life, the biddy has had strong opinions about how things should be. By the time she achieves biddyhood, these have become less like individual preferences and more like laws of nature. Concurrently, a lifetime of caution and keeping up appearances seems to become an annoyance of which she decides she has had enough.

It has always been a good idea not to get in the biddy's way, but it is now more than a good idea. It is a necessary survival technique.

THE BIDDY AND THE TRAFFIC COP

The inexperienced officer believes that the law is sacrosanct and must be enforced equally across the citizenry. He will, therefore, pull the biddy over and attempt to explain to her that green means go, and other motorists expect her to do that or something like it; that she is supposed to keep her car between the lines rather than over one of them; and that the 35 mph limit was not intended for the fast lane of the freeway.

More seasoned members of the force know that, if stopped, the biddy will argue that whatever the color of the light, there's no point in her going until she has remembered which way she wants to go; that as far as their precious lines are concerned, they are only painted on and so should be taken as general guidelines — suggestions, really — rather than hard and fast rules; and that 35 mph is quite fast enough for any decent person. And more importantly, they should stop harassing her and wasting taxpayers' money when there are thousands of hard-core criminals roaming the streets this very minute. They should let her go on her way and after twenty minutes of listening to her rant, *all* of the officers do.

WELL-TRAVELED BIDDY

The biddy's favorite mode of travel is the cruise ship. This is probably because of the wide variety of available entertainment and recreation, which ranges from eating, drinking, and dressing up to dressing up for the purpose of eating and drinking, and of course, drinking in preparation for dressing up for eating. Thanks to such events as "South Sea Island Mai

Tai Night," or the "Si, Si, Sombrero Margarita Mixer," the biddy is able to absorb all the local culture anyone could want without ever leaving the ship at all – which is fine with her, since, unaccountably, they tend to stop in some pretty unsavory neighborhoods.

Similarly, the biddy on land is known to frequent airport security checkpoints, though she has no ticket, no destination, and no apparent intention to board a plane. To the casual observer this may appear to be a pointless exercise. But it seems that the biddy craves the attention, and is somehow just as gratified by her tenth security check as she was by her first.

THE BIDDY AND THE BUS TOUR

Those who have spoken to biddys after one of their semi-annual bus tours have noticed, no doubt, that they are fuzzy on the details of where they went and what they saw. The reason for this is to be found in the conversations of the biddys themselves as they are boarding the bus, while they are on the bus, and as they disembark the bus. These exchanges have nothing to do with where they have been or where they are going. They have, on the other hand, everything to do with what Irene could have been thinking when she decided to wear those shoes; why Cynthia seems to have required the presence of the appliance repairman eleven times in the last month, and certain facts relevant to the previous employment of the new minister, whose sermons never have seemed quite on the mark.

In other words, the value of the bus tour to the biddy is not that it will take her somewhere, but rather that it is an extended period during which she can engage in her favorite pastime with a minimum of distractions.

Anyway, as every biddy knows — and will be quick to tell you — if you've seen one Gothic cathedral you've pretty much seen them all.

Biddy with a Cane

Sooner or later, every biddy contemplates the acquisition of a cane – but not for the reasons one might think. The biddy, after all, is no fool. She knows as well as anyone that a cane is worse than useless as an aid to balance or perambulation. If you doubt this, try going down a steep stairway with a forty-pound purse on one arm while leaning on a cane with the other.

On the other hand, there's nothing like a cane for imparting a certain dignity and hauteur to one's persona – particularly if one's persona is the tiniest bit wobbly to begin with. So the biddy who equips herself with a cane does so initially for the sole purpose of making herself a more impressive personage (see facing page). Soon, however, she discovers that it has a number of practical uses she had not thought of before (see following pages). These, of course, do not include walking.

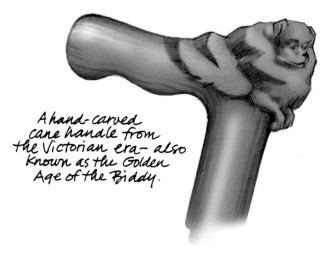

A hand-carved
cane handle from
the Victorian era- also
Known as the Golden
Age of the Biddy.

The biddy without a cane is dressed in a somewhat ordinary fashion, and she contemplates a steep stairway with obvious trepidation. This biddy lacks conviction that the stairs can be maneuvered successfully.

The biddy with the cane has greater style, improved posture, and the knowledge that she need only wait for someone to carry her down the stairs.

ANCILLARY USES OF THE CANE

Reach Extension

Doorstop

Service
Provider

Anti Cab-Stealing Device

PASTIMES

SHOPPING, LUNCH, FLOWER
SHOWS. OR HOW ABOUT SHOPPING, LUNCH,
AND A FLOWER SHOW?

STAYING SHARP

The biddy has reached a stage of life when she is relieved of many of the activities which occupied her younger years, such as cooking, housekeeping, and childrearing. This new era means she is free to indulge in the one activity she really cares about: chatting. However, a lifetime of multi-tasking has left her constitutionally unable to do one thing at a time without feeling that she is slacking shamefully. So for the biddy, bingo is not a game, it is an essential mental exercise and a good thing to be doing at her age, especially if the biddy happens to be talking about that unfortunate incident involving Frieda's daughter and the produce man at the Bag'n'Save at the same time she is marking off numbers on her bingo cards.

THE FLOWER SHOW

If you ever have occasion to seek the company or counsel of a biddy – if, for instance, you want to know how long to cook a four-pound rump roast, or where to find an addition to your collection of porcelain owls – there is one place where you cannot fail to find one, and usually en masse. We are referring to the flower show: an event which, like the rodeo or *bierfest*, seems to be taking place somewhere at any given moment and, for the true aficionado, needs no reason. We will not take up the reader's time explaining the nature of the flower show, because after it is said that there are flowers and they are shown, there is little to add. The point is that it is the one venue where you can be certain of locating a biddy, and where you need have no fear of embarrassment due to mistaken biddy identification.

Because if she's female and she's at a flower show, she's a biddy.

The Secret of Shopping

Everyone knows that the biddy and the shopping trip go together like a set of Limoges and a crocheted tea cozy. But the more experienced observer knows that, where the biddy is concerned, shopping is not quite what it seems. Like her male counterpart, the

coot, the biddy doesn't need much and there is no particular place she has to be. But unlike the coot (who travels aimlessly and alone, and never buys anything), the biddy travels in groups and buys everything in sight. The next day, the same group travels the exact route in reverse and returns everything.

Ingeniously, this acquisition (and subsequent rejection of unneeded merchandise) gives the illusion that the group's gathering has some actual purpose – not just once, but twice.

Then they have lunch.

THE BOOK CLUB

The biddy, being no fool, understands that advancing age does not mean one should stop improving one's mind. This accounts for the founding of such institutions as the Book Club. But the biddy, being no bluenose, also understands that improving one's mind does not preclude having a good time. This accounts for the amount of wine which is consumed at every meeting of the Book Club, which in turn may account for the fact that some biddy book clubs have been known to read and discuss the same book as many as six or eight times without any members noticing. In fact, one such club has adopted as its motto a quotation from Tolstoy, which goes, "If you got wine, who needs a @#**##! book?"

Or maybe it was Hemingway.

THE BIDDY AND THE SPIRIT WORLD

The biddy has an obvious affinity for almost every sort of paranormal activity. No biddy's home would be complete without at least one deck of tarot cards and a Ouija board, and every biddy's routine includes regular consultations with her psychic and her astrologer.

This is commonly attributed to the biddy's naivete and gullibility, and most members of her family shrug off her frequent forays into the netherworld as harmless foibles. But often the biddy has a clear and definite purpose, such as the example of Mrs. Flora Baines Anderson McVeach, shown at right, who has vowed not to rest until she has brought her late third husband, Reginald Tandy McVeach, back from the Other Side for at least a few hours.

Because she wasn't finished with him and he knows it.

THE KEEPER OF ORDER

APPARENTLY THERE ARE STILL SOME
PEOPLE WHO ARE UNFAMILIAR WITH THE
FUNCTION OF "THE DRINK COASTER"

KEEPING THEM IN LINE

Every biddy knows that somewhere, at any given moment, a doily or slipcover is out of place, a child's nose needs attention, a young girl's skirt is too short or hair needs a good brushing, a glass is not on a coaster, a blueberry stain is about to set, and someone's feet are on the furniture.

The biddy knows these things will not be corrected without benefit of her influence – or better yet – her direct participation.

She is not stingy with either.

Keeping it Presentable

The biddy is a person of delicate sensibilities, and she assumes that others are the same – or if they are not, then it is her duty to elevate their standards for them. For this reason, the typical biddy has spent the better part of her life attempting to hide, minimize, disguise, or ignore the less attractive aspects of everyday life. This accounts for such phenomena as the cat litter box with Swiss chalet-style roof, the plug-in room deodorizer, the fuzzy toilet seat cover, and the many cashmere sweaters and tasteful neckties she bought for her husband.

One might imagine that this compulsion would have run its course by the time she actually reached biddyhood, but that does not seem to be the case. On the contrary, it seems that the biddy simply continues to raise the bar in terms of what is and is not suitable for the eyes of decent people to behold.

Yesterday the toilet brush; today the toaster.

Ceramic
Tissue Box Cover

Crocheted
Toaster Cover

Clown
Paper Towel
Cover

Crocheted
Tea Cozy with
Rhinestones

Wishing Well
Wastebasket
Enhancer

Cork, Pipe Cleaner,
and Taffeta Ballerina
Dish Soap Cover

Plastic Ivy
Toilet Brush Prettifier

Keeping Them on Their Toes

The biddy does not think of the waiter as a server, but rather as an eternal challenge. Before she even enters the room, she knows he is going to seat her at a drafty table, bring her tepid coffee and wilted salad, purposely substitute a pasta side dish for the spring vegetables she ordered, and attempt to charge her for the dessert he served to the adjacent table. Furthermore, she knows that he knows that she knows, and so it is imperative that she gain the upper hand from the very beginning. This is why the biddy fixes the waiter with a steely gaze before he has even pulled out a chair or offered a menu, never answers his questions without first looking him up and down appraisingly, and always sends at least one dish back for essentially no reason.

The wily waiter will often make a show of innocence, as if he genuinely had no idea what could be wrong with the old bat at table five.

The biddy is not fooled.

KEEPING THINGS SAFE

The biddy is aware of many undesirable and dangerous activities that seem somehow to escape the attention of the general population. She therefore recognizes that it is her solemn duty to keep an eye out for roaming gangs of feral children, neighborhood canvassers with sinister-looking clipboards, so-called "delivery" people, and a host of other suspicious characters who are obviously up to no good. The more experienced and conscientious biddy keeps a notepad near her station at the window, on which she records license numbers, approximate time of day, detailed physical descriptions, and her personal theory of what the potential perps are up to. When the pad is full, she passes this helpful information on to the police, whose appreciation of her assistance knows no bounds. This is demonstrated by the fact that she and the cops are often on a first-name basis.

BOSOM BIDDYS

It matters little what road
you take. The important thing is the
company along the way

WHAT THE BIDDY KNOWS

The biddy doesn't know how — or for that matter, why — one would put oil into a car engine. She doesn't know what good cell phones are, since it is obvious that none of them turn on properly anyhow. She doesn't know what ever happened to good manners and good service, and she probably doesn't know that her skirt is tucked into the waistband of her slip. But she knows one thing: an hour with a friend (and maybe a little drop of wine) is the true measure of wealth.

THE BIDDY AND THE MEANING OF LIFE

Many aspects of the biddy's behavior suggest that she may have come to the aforementioned conclusion before actually departing the physical world. But once she has become an observer rather than a participant in the everyday ups and downs of life on earth, it is a certainty that she has learned one thing: if you want to fly, you'd better be able to take yourself lightly.

Cathy